LANDSCAPING

FOR BEGINNERS

ALSO BY ERIC JASON

Container Gardening

https://getbook.at/ContainerbyEric

Greenhouse Gardening

https://getbook.at/GreenhousebyEric

Hydroponics for Beginners

https://getbook.at/HydroponicsbyEric

Raised Bed Gardening for Beginners

https://getbook.at/RaisedbedbyEric

Table of Contents

INTRODUCTION

The art of landscaping has to take into account the total environment of every development and then restructure it with natural elements such as shrubs, landform, trees, and water to create appealing and pleasant scenery. Rather than causing destruction to the environment, it makes a notable contribution to its development.

Landscaping is more than just beautifying your yard. A well-maintained lawn can make an ordinary open yard look attractive. Landscape design has to do with changing your garden into an appealing retreat while reducing the impacts of human activities on the environment and plants in your garden. While incorporating some potted plants helps enhance your garden's beauty, the real value of landscaping goes beyond aesthetic improvements.

The benefits humans derive from interacting with grass, trees, and plants are well researched and documented. A study has established that people can be relieved from stress and healed when they interact with nature. When working in environments with grass and plants, employees are more productive and have improved cognitive function. Also, children with ADHD seem to have a better focus after being outdoors.

However, apart from what science says, what people instinctively feel about the green spaces and plants is more important. Individuals also testify that greenery makes their lives better, and they will try to incorporate it into their lives.

According to Husqvarna Global Golden Reports of 2012, 63 percent of respondents stated that they would pay more for a house or apartment situated in a neighborhood with high-quality green spaces. While 34 percent will pay more for a location with excellent shopping and 33 percent are willing to opt for good cultural value.

CHAPTER ONE: A GENERAL OVERVIEW OF LANDSCAPING

What is Landscaping?

Landscaping can be described as any activity that is meant to modify the visible features of a portion of land as well as its living objects. It can also be defined as the art and craft of cultivating plants with the aim of creating a picturesque environment within the landscape area.

Landscape gardening refers to an aesthetic aspect of horticulture that has to do with the growing of ornamental plants to create an appealing effect in the surrounding. We can also describe landscape gardening as beautifying a piece of land with a house or other object of interest. Landscaping is being designed to create a picturesque view by planting shrubs, trees, and lawns. It has to do with the imitation of nature in the garden and the improvement of the community's whole living environment.

The landscape expression can be quiet, retired, bold, gay, and so on. This expression should be in conformity to the environment and purpose. It ought to be a picture and not just a compilation of interesting things. As landscaping has to do with creating a striking effect on the land with plants and other substances, the landscape designer should have at least a little knowledge of the art, physiology, ecology, and ornamental gardening. He should also have some experience in architecture to understand the relationship between plant form, buildings, and color.

Factors affecting the landscape design

Many factors are affecting the creation an ideal design for a particular location. These factors include:

The human choice: Making his surroundings comfortable and living pleasurable is the man's ultimate desire. His selection of plants and creating design is good evidence. For that reason, different techniques of gardening have come into existence,

Site: Location is a crucial factor that affects landscaping as a suitable design is made according to it. The site is chosen according to plan, in a formal style gardening. The site's topography also has effects on the design.

Heritage: Man inherits the sense of aesthetic and botany knowledge and utilizes them accordingly. Our rich heritage teaches us to use fragrant trees and flowers to improve the environment.

Climate: The climatic condition of an area affects the choice of plant material accordingly. Suitable plant material should be selected according to climate.

Soil: Ideally, plants should be selected according to the characteristics of soil types.

Views: Viewing the valley, woods, hills, and mountains, etc. from a distance are preferred from the garden location.

Natural Elements of Landscape

Different kinds of landscape depend on the prevailing agro-climate and geographical conditions which characterize the earth. There are streams, swamps, lakes, mountains, deserts, plains, forests, rivers, seas, valleys, glens, hills, etc, which comprise a significant natural landscape element. When there is an accord between natural elements like vegetation, ground forms and animal life at specific points, such landscape areas are attractive and express the mood or feeling of the landscape attribute like admiration, exhilaration, cheeriness, or sadness. There are several qualities of natural landscape beauty, such as the majestic, the picturesque, the graceful, the idyllic, the delicate, the serene, the bold, and so on. Man has imitated the natural components for enhancing the landscape in his surroundings and transformed certain areas in the garden form for his pleasure.

Some Significant Landscape Gardening Terms

Axis: Axis is an imaginary line that separates the garden into two fractions. It also links two or more points. It's structured in the form of a path line of trees or fountains, and so on. It is called the central axis when it divides the garden into two equal parts. Axis is central in a formal style while it is oblique in an informal style. This axis controls the movement in the garden from the point of entry to the terminal end. An axis in the garden is dominating, orderly, or directional.

Symmetrical plan: In a symmetrical arrangement, various objects are on either side of an axis or in balance about a central point. A formal plan or symmetrical plan is synonymous with prettiness and is attractive and pleasant. The reason for this is that the symmetry is to be allied with plan clarity, unity, balance, rhythm, and so on. The symmetrical plan is disciplined and precise; it necessitates accuracy in maintenance and detail and boldness.

Dynamic Symmetry: In this kind of symmetric plan, each of the poles creates its magnetic field, and there is a field of dynamic tension between the two fields.

Asymmetrical Plan: Symmetry is absent on both sides of the axis in these plans, but harmony, unity, and balance are maintained.

Circulation in Landscaping: Circulation means a pathway from the entry point to the terminal end in landscape gardening. This varies with topography and the landscaping style. A garden with more circulation patterns would have more points of view and attraction.

Vista: Vista is a dominant component of the feature or three dimensional confined view of the terminal building. It can be human-made or natural. Natural vistas are very common around the snowy peaks and lofty mountains. The characteristics of vistas will be its overall effect. It will induce motion or be calm.

CHAPTER TWO: BENEFITS OF LANDSCAPING

Landscape gardening isn't only aesthetic, which is intended to make places look beautiful but also essential and functional. The environments we live in make a considerable contribution to our quality of life. The term 'landscape' doesn't only signify beautiful scenery but also connotes a rich historical record of natural features, modified by the people's activities over the years. It represents the context with which we base our everyday lives, reflecting in our literature, painting, and music.

Environmental Benefits of Landscaping

Natural Coolants: Lawns are very much cooler than cement or asphalt. Grass acts as an "air-conditional" for the environment. Indeed, grasses can be twenty degrees cooler than soil and thirty-one degrees cooler than asphalt. In addition, trees shading houses can lower attic temperatures by about forty degrees.

Environmental Cleaners: Grasses play a significant role when it comes to capturing smoke particles, dust, and other pollutants. Lawns also produce oxygen.

Water Protectors: A well-maintained lawns absorb unhealthful run-off that may otherwise filter into bodies of water.

Air Cleaners: Healthy glasses soak up carbon dioxide and break it down into carbon and oxygen. In reality, a lawn of 50 x 50 feet produces sufficient oxygen for a family of four.

Noise Reducer: Plants and lawns significantly reduce noise pollution; they are capable of reducing noise levels by twenty percent to thirty percent more than hard surfaces like pavement or concrete.

Home turf holds back and absorbs run-off into bodies of water. Even in neighborhoods experiencing drought and have water restrictions, landscapes and lawns must remain a feasible part of healthy environments.

A number of sustainable practices will enable a managed lawns and landscapes to reduce water usage but still provide important environmental benefits.

Benefits of Urban Landscaping

Several kinds of research have demonstrated how essential it is to incorporate parks and tree canopies into towns and cities. And their results have found that they supply a number of lifestyle benefits that improve the well-being of the inhabitants.

Tree Canopies and Parks Help Reduce Noise

A recent study by the United States Forest Service established that districts with tree-lined streets and larger yard trees recorded low crime rates. Studies also reveal that mere viewing trees and plants, even through a window, will reduce stress and lower blood pressure.

According to a study by Marc Berman of the University of Michigan, taking a walk in a serene environment with trees and plants, even when situated in the center of a city, has been found to improve memory and attention.

According to a study conducted by Housley and Wolf, neighborhoods that include community green spaces, experience minimal occurrences of stress, enjoy a lower cost of healthcare, and enjoy an improved quality of life as a result.

Commercial Benefits of Landscaping

Studies have shown that when clients are provided with plants inside buildings and landscaped vicinities around buildings, businesses tend to be more successful. A study confirmed 7% increased rental rates for commercial offices with top quality landscapes.

Buyers claimed that they could spend nine to twelve percent extra for goods and services in central commercial areas with top quality tree canopies.

Shoppers pointed out that they can travel a long distance to visit and spend more time in a location with top quality tree canopies.

Businesses and companies that provide an avenue for their workers to interact with nature also benefit. According to a study by Rachael Kaplan, Ph.D., employees who can sight nature right from their desks enjoyed much more job satisfaction, happiness, and improved health.

Physical and Psychological Benefits of Landscaping

- **Prevents Erosion on Your Property**

In every yard, erosion poses a threat. As rain and wind move across your garden, this can shift the soil away from the garden beds and plants. Rocks may become dislodged in steep areas, posing a threat to the safety of your family. A good structure landscape design will help prevent erosion, particularly in steep areas, when retaining walls are being used. The retaining walls can be functional while also attractive. Be functional by holding the soil firm in its place and, at the same time, providing a pleasant framework for sculptures and plants.

- **Divide Large Spaces into Alluring Nooks**

When you have ample space, creating private areas where your neighbors cannot have access may be difficult. But with landscape design, you can easily divide a large garden into secluded, yet appealing areas.

A well-structured landscape can include an outdoor living room framed by shrubs or trees to restrain the neighborhood's noise and bring about a feeling of being out in nature. In creating the landscape design, you will consider how you intend to make use of the space in order to make a perfect environment and background that suit your needs and imaginations.

- **Prevents Flooding in Your Yard**

When the rains come in the spring and fall, your garden can turn into a mud pit if you don't have a solid landscaping plan. The existing landscape design and plants in your garden can be damaged if you experience floods. And this can make the space unusable. A perfect design should direct run-off and storm-water to a designated drainage area and diverts them away from your plants. If a storm damages your existing design, Architectural Landscape Design will assist in restoring its original look and make any necessary alterations to prevent any future occurrence of flooding.

- **Reduce Air Pollutants**

With landscape design, you will embrace nature in a predictable and manicured way, and then derive other benefits from plants. When you include plentiful amounts of foliage, the air quality around your home will improve. Greeneries absorb harmful chemicals and pollutants, decontaminating the air without using machinery or electricity. Landscaping features may be as productive as you desire, but the number of plants you have will determine the number of pollutants they will absorb.

- **Proliferate Local Ecosystem**

You do not need to plan a high-maintenance landscape design. Many plans make use of grasses and local plants to create an attractive garden that will flourish from one season to another. Suppose a design utilizes native plants of the region. In that case, the handling of landscaping areas during seasonal changes will require no extra attention and care from you or the landscaping crew. Changes in temperatures, average rainfall, and soil are capable of posing a challenge to non-native foliage. At the same time, most of the native plants receive all their needed nutrients from the local topsoil without adding chemical fertilizers. Moreover, any design that mimics the natural environment will tempt squirrels, birds, and other small critters to make their home.

- **Treats Your Space as an Eco-System**

Your garden or yard is not just a place to relax after a long and hectic day; it is an eco-system on its own. The sunny spots, shaded areas, and changing land slope have their varied needs that should be weighed up before accommodating them. A high-quality landscape design will consider these factors and treat your garden or yard as an eco-system, putting the right plants in the correct position. The outcome of this is a design that plans for erosion, drainage, and sustainable plant-life.

- **Reduces Impact on Environment**

When you are planting a flowerbed without a landscape design, you may include plants and flowers that aren't suitable to your region's weather conditions. To make up for the effects of conditions, humidity, and soil type of your garden, you might need to add fertilizer to the soil. Nearly all store-bought fertilizers contain chemicals that can damage the environments, though they help tropical foliage blossom during summer months.

When it rains, the leftover fertilizer in the soil finds its way into the water source, posing a threat to native plants and wildlife. With every project, landscape design puts sustainability first. While you can use your preferred tropical plants in one area of the design, you will not use them all over the place. Therefore, reducing the use of non-native and exotic plants limits the impact of landscaping on the environment.

Benefits of Plants in Landscape Gardening

- Plants that represent a significant constituent in landscape design help reduce environmental pollution and lessen some of the effects of air, wind, sound, heat, and so on.

- During the process of photosynthesis, plants absorb carbon dioxide, therefore releasing oxygen and purifying the air.

- Plants that have thick foliage also trap pollutants, which are being washed away when it rains.

- Several plants such as, hyacinth, mustard, and hydrangea, absorb poisonous substances from their surroundings.

- Plants can channel, guide, diffuse, or block winds. Plants could be utilized to direct wind so that it flushes out the pollutants in the air.

- Erosion caused by too much rain, wind, or snow is controlled by plants. Some plants with fibrous surface roots, deep root systems, and good branching also reduce the loss of fertile topsoil.

- Plants bring down temperature by reducing the radiated heat.

- The deciduous trees shielding their leaves during winter give room to lights to pass through, thus keep the space warm.

CHAPTER THREE: LANDSCAPING PRINCIPLES

Here are the general principles of landscaping:

An ideal landscape garden is like a perfect landscape painting that expresses some thoughts or feelings. Its expression may be gay, bold, retired, quiet, etc.

Utility and beauty must be harmoniously combined. This means we should divide the area into different parts, and there should be a conceived plan for each part. The entire plan ought to be something the viewer catches the overall purpose and effect of the plan without having to stop to analyze its components. The simplicity of design must be the target when executing the plan. A good landscape design must have open space.

Allow the building and garden to merge into each other. There shouldn't be stopping suddenly, especially in front of the house. The garden should be beautiful when viewing from the doors and windows. Planting around the house, climbers on the porch and against the wall, decoration of rooms and verandah with hanging baskets, flowering plants, and attractive foliage serve to unique the garden. Every portion of the property must be designed such that it gives an astonishing effect to the guests. One must avoid overcrowding of plants and objects.

The Art principles of landscaping

Making pictures with plant material is what landscaping entails; therefore, its principles are very similar to those of art. Here are the principles:

Rhythm: Rhythm is referred to as the repetition of the same object at equidistance. This could be created through shapes, a continuous line movement or progression of sizes, rhythm creates eye movement. Usually, in gardens, a single tree species with uniform shape and height are planted to produce this effect. Water canals and fountains have also been widely used to create such effects in Mogul gardens. In recent times, other objects like lights are used as well to create the rhythm effect.

Balance: Maintaining a balance on both sides of the central line is very important. The principle of making a balance in the see-saw game will assist in understanding this. You can balance equal weight only when they're equidistant from the center. In the case of unequal weights, the heavier ought to move towards the center for making balance. The balance can be symmetrical, informal, or formal types. It will distract the attention and appear crooked, if unbalanced. Their texture, form, color, and so on is kept in view when making the balance with the plants.

Emphasis or Accent: To avoid a monotonous view, the emphasis or accent is created in the gardens. The purpose of this technique is to stress the vital things. It is also considered as the center of attraction. Typically, unusual objects such as statues, trees, tall fountains, etc. are utilized to create the emphasis or accent effect. Statues have been widely used to create such effects in English gardens.

Contrast: This principle is especially helpful in emphasizing the most excellent features of an object. You can understand this easily by following the contrast color theory. A speckle of scarlet color will contrast and makes scarlet color exceptional against the green background. This is very common in nature. You can also make use of other contrast colors. Some of the other examples that can be followed include weeping growth habit against upright growth, rough texture against soft texture, dwarf against tall, etc. It must be done in such a way that one of the two different objects or plants have dominance over the other. This way, one serves as a supporting background while the other becomes a feature. The contrasting objects of equal power can bring about visual tensions.

Proportion; Proportion here is referred to as the relation of one thing to another in magnitude. These are established when two or more objects are placed together. In landscaping, shrubbery border, herbaceous borders, buildings, trees, paths, space allotted for lawn, and other objects must be in the right proportion. This will create a harmonious picturesque effect. You can notice such effects in Mogul and Persian gardens. Proportion assists in organizing space while out of proportion portion of land in the garden can distract attention.

Harmony This is referred to as an overall effect of various features, color scheme, and style of the entire scenery. The level of unity or harmony of different landscape components is a measure induced in us and is called beauty. So, we can define beauty as the manifest relationship of every part of something observed. The harmonious effect is achieved when different components of the landscape are rightly placed. Landscapes of such create a beautiful effect and appeal to visitors, while a lack of unity or absence of harmony is ugliness.

CHAPTER FOUR: LANDSCAPE GARDEN STYLES

There have been changes periodically in garden style with new ideas and necessities. Generally, garden styles are grouped into three categories, which are formal style, informal style, and freestyle of gardening. Therefore, different garden styles such as, cottage garden, French gardens, Mediterranean gardens, traditional gardens, Japanese gardens, English gardens modern garden, etc. are sub categories of these three categories.

Formal Garden Style: The main characteristic of formal style is that initially, the plan is put on the paper, and afterward, the site is chosen accordingly. The plan here is symmetrical. This category of gardens is a geometric design that is rectangular or squarish. So, roads and paths are cut at the right angle. Beds for flowers are also in geometric shapes. They have some kind of enclosure. Shrubs and trees are necessarily arranged geometrical and kept in shape by training and trimming. Other features such as cascades, water pools, fountains, and so on are used for further attraction. Mogul gardens and Persian gardens are examples of such gardening.

Informal Garden Style: This garden's style mirrors the naturalistic effect of total scenery and symbolizes natural beauty. The informal style is just the opposite of formal style. Here, the plan is asymmetrical and also according to the available land for creating a garden. Paths and roads are bending and curvaceous. Hillocks are set to form a natural mountainous view. Water bodies are made of asymmetrical shapes. Beds for flowers are made of irregular shapes to suit the environment. Plants are allowed to grow in natural form, and annual pruning is carried out instead of trimming. The best example of this gardening style is Japanese gardens.

Free Garden Style: This style of gardening combines the functional aspects of informal and formal style. An example of freestyle of gardening is the Rose garden of Ludhiana.

Here are the descriptions of some of the garden styles you can choose from:

1. Cottage Garden Style

Cottage garden's plants are diverse and colorful; they have the propensity to spread out into paths and lawns. Cottage gardens are filled with an array of plants and flowers that are both practical and beautiful. This garden-style features colorful ornamental, edible, herb, and medicinal plants all combined as one. Every available space is utilized in plantings to create a feeling of charm and "organized mess."

Cottage style of garden is the relaxed and sometimes disorderly progeny of the highly uptight formal garden. Also, in the cottage garden style, less emphasis is placed on plants' symmetry or arrangement. This garden style is beautiful and striking, but it could be a bit challenging to get it right as it involves least rules. When you fill your garden with the flower, plants, colors, and scents you love, it becomes a source of joy and happiness.

Elements of cottage garden Styles

- Informal plantings placed at random with very small open space

- Fences and walls covered with vines and climbing plants

- Natural objects such as decomposed stone, gravel, mulch, and brick used for pathways

- Edible plants combined with ornamental and medicinal plants

Ideal Plants for Cottage Garden Styles

Cottage garden plants are exotic and not uncommon. Most shrubs and flowering perennials are suitable American natives, and common species are part of them. Some traditional flowering shrubs like lilacs, roses, hydrangeas, and trees like magnolias fit well in this look. Clematis, popularly known as the "Queen of climbers" is an attractive flowering vine that comes in different colors and bloom times. Clematis is a perfect choice for growing over trees, walls, and even on top of other plants in a cottage garden. Cornflowers and Shasta daisies are great for this garden style too. Creeping Phlox is a beautiful groundcover that attracts bees and butterflies, whereas flooring your landscape with scented pink, white, and blue flowers. I wonder how you will see any of these wonderful plants and not smile!

In addition, incorporate edible plants and herbs into your cottage garden. Add in lavender, sweet bay, rosemary, pomegranates, grapes, figs, blueberry, and sage with your ornamental plants for a cottage garden look, scent, and fantastic taste.

2. Traditional Garden Style

This is the ideal garden for French, Italian, and colonial inspired architecture as it focuses on symmetry and balance. In this garden style, spaces are dominated by green lawns that are balanced by green shrubs and green trees. Traditional gardens are typically not packed with color. Often you will see these gardens making use of only white as an accent color. If you love the symmetry and balance presented by traditional garden style but do not want your own to be so "upright,' surely you can borrow formal garden design elements to add into your garden. Traditional gardens do not have to be so strict. Some designers of the garden will put cottage gardens in the same category as traditional garden styles.

Elements of traditional gardens

- Framed views of stone fountains, cleanly edged walkways, rows of orderly clipped hedges, and perfectly trimmed lawn

- Symmetry by repeating the same plantings on both sides of the walkway or path

- The straight path, straight lines, and bold geometric forms

- Formal hedges pruned into rhythmic shapes

- Horizontal spreads of green manicured lawn

Plants for traditional garden styles

Columnar trees like "Hi" Yew and "Blue Arrow" Juniper, and boxwood shrubs since hedging are all autographs of the traditional garden style. Tulips, peonies, and roses each symbolize a different feature of this strong floral heritage. Hardy "Orange Emperor" Tulips, "Coral Supreme" Peony, and rambling groundcover Apricot Drift Rose are my favorites.

3. Modern Garden Style

Each generation has a tendency to get a bit trendier. Therefore, as cottage gardens are still a popular garden style choice, the contemporary/modern gardens have grown in popularity. As it is now, the modern garden styles still have one foot in the past. Some traditional elements are present – there are still abundant plantings but less chaotic than cottage garden style, so managing it is easier. However, unlike the traditional garden, the underlying designs of modern gardens are informal. The symmetry of geometric shapes is substituted with asymmetrical in this garden style.

The modern garden styles ultimately morphed into contemporary garden styles due to their similarities. The modern style is all about minimalism, smooth surfaces, and clean lines. The choices of plants are reduced to a few essential assortments. The design is stripped back, and hard surfaces materials prevail over plantings. The contemporary garden style focuses on entertainment and leisure with the "outdoor room" being its focal point.

Elements of modern garden Styles

- Metal, be it sheet metal, metal grids, or even galvanizes steel will assist in carrying out the modern look of this garden style

- Planters or architectural sculptures made from ceramic, resin, or concrete in bold or grey colors are an excellent choice to imitate and contrast the shapes in your modern garden.

- Water features like fountains and ponds with geometric shapes and clean lines are a staple in modern garden style.

CHAPTER FIVE: LANDSCAPING
TIPS AND IDEAS

If you have never attempted a landscape design before, you can be overwhelmed by all the available options. However, thinking of it as a room inside your home can make it very simple. You can use the same principles that guide you to setup a room inside as a guide to design your outdoors as well. Since you can put a room together easily, creating a landscape shouldn't be a problem for you. Here are some vital landscape design tips to help you:

Determine Landscape Needs and Wants

Prepare your list of needs and wants. Do you need a play space for your kids? Do you want to grow fruit and vegetables? Do you want a patio where your family would gather? Make rough sketches of your garden and decide on where you want things to be placed; this is a great landscape design principle for the newbie. They do not have to be master plans; you can easily play around with ideas without much commitment and time.

Know the Purpose of Your Garden

In history, all gardens were designed with one of these three purposes, to be visually picturesque, to create space, or to raise food. So, by knowing the goals you want your garden to accomplish, you can prepare a space for dual purpose, for example, combining edible plants with ornamentals in a single planting bed.

Consider the Location of Your Property

Study the patterns of wind and sun. You may intend to site a patio on the western side of the building that will receive a lot of daylight sun, but the implication of this is that dinner in August would be hot. And also, a fire pit will be quickly extinguished by the wind whistling around a corner. These are mistakes commonly made by most beginners to landscape design. Your plan must consider what the wind and sun offer at different times of the day, month, and year.

Know the Peculiarities of Your Property

Every portion of land has its own distinctive set of features: soil conditions, mature shrubs, existing trees, windy spots, shade, sunny areas, and changes in elevation that might not go with your neighbor's. Learn to understand the topography and microclimates of your property. Run a test on your soil to know if it is acidic and study its composition to see if it is heavy and clayish or sandy and loose. The more you are acquainted with your property's characteristics, the better advantage you have on its best personalities.

Take Advantage of Borrowed Views

Do not be shy about making the most of the beauty that surrounds your property. Have you been seeing a glorious tree that turns bright red in autumn in your neighbor's garden? To make your garden feel more expansive, add in borrowed loveliness into your landscape. Do not block the sight with a high fence.

Select the Proper Dimensions for a Walkway or Path

If it's a tight space, you can lay out a path that is as narrow as eighteen inches. However, the broader the path, the more spacious your garden will be. If you have enough space, you can create a forty-eight inches wide pathway, with which two people can walk beside each other. You can as well make a curve or experiment with a layout pathway that narrows and widens to create visual attention.

Create a Focal Point

For a garden design to be great, it must have a focal point or sequence of focal points, and this principle is easy to incorporate into a landscape design. It can be a stunning plant or a sculpture, a series of shrubs or trees, let it be something that draws your eyes around the landscape.

Place a Patio Based on How You Want to Utilize the Space

Decide whether you prefer to utilize your patio as an outdoor dining room and ensure it is well-located to your kitchen. Also, consider having a private area to sit and read a book. Place a patio at the garden's edge and turn it into a secret by planting a hedge around it.

Select Plants that Will Flourish in Your Microclimate

Grow plants that are well suited to your region in your garden. The obvious choices are Native plants. You can also take note o f plants that thrive in your neighbor's yards. Bear in mind that your garden has microclimates of shade and sun, and choose plants accordingly.

Start Small

Among the principles of creating a magnificent landscape is gradually implementing your plan and making the process pleasurable. From your rough sketches or master plan, begin with maybe a small flower bed. Go out and work on it for a few hours when you are less busy and don't bother yourself about filling up everything at once. You should take your time so you do not eventually get too sloppy with your landscaping project. Also live with your landscape design for a while, after you have spent more time outside, you will begin to notice spots where you prefer to go and relax with which you would not have seen at the start.

Plant for a Tree's Future

Think about the shape and size a tree would be at maturity when planting it. It's very depressing in a garden to see branches of a tree hack off as it gets too big for its location. Provide ample space for a tree to grow as wide and high as it wants so your future generations can enjoy its beauty.

CHAPTER SIX: CREATING EDIBLE LANDSCAPE DESIGNS

Several vast, fertile farming lands are wasted nowadays on the cultivation of shrubs and lawns. Bounty and beauty can flourish together if you spend your time in designing a multifunctional edible landscape. The concept of edible landscape is very deep; there are several options and variations to explore. The American residents cover millions of productive agricultural lands around their houses with marigold, lawn, wisteria, and azalea beds, and an occasional maple or privet. Yet this land can equally be used to grow beautiful edible plants, so that property owners can produce a substantial amount of bounty in their gardens – a much more proficient way to use soil.

The lawn areas can be minimized by putting decorative borders of striking paprika peppers, rainbow chard, and herbs can be placed in the place of the typical landscape. Blueberries that are decorative year-round can be grown in the place of the short-lived color of spring azaleas. Also, you can grow plum and pear trees that have yellow fall foliage, decorative fruits, and a spring show of flowers. These plants are

55

not just attractive; they offer delicious fruit and could save you money.

Edible landscaping is the practice that involves combining edible gardening with landscape design. Yes, you can own a beautiful garden while also eat from it! Indeed, it is a bit challenging using edible plants in garden design and making it look beautiful. Scraggly peppers that usually have naked stems, chaotic tomatoes, sprawling squash vines, for example, are why a lot of vegetables are being grown at the farthest end of the backyard – usually placed out of sight in a few garden beds.

Edible Plants can look beautiful.

It is a great thing to note that this popular puzzle isn't a proof to conclude that edible plants are unattractive. In reality, an edible garden can compete with the best winners of the Chelsea Garden Show. In fact, several edible gardens have won at Chelsea!

Apart from the fact that the edible landscape is a viable design option, it is the most compelling landscape idea for the future if maintained with organic methods. The incredible benefits of edible landscapes cannot be overemphasized; they include:

Energy Saving: Crop from your garden calls for no shipping, no or little refrigeration, and less energy for plowing, planting, spraying, and harvesting the bounty.

Food Safety: You are acquainted with the chemicals (if any) you make use of, and you will not combine huge batches of vegetables. So, they cannot contaminate one another.

Water Savings: Studies have made it known that most home growers make use of less than 50 percent of the water farming production needs to produce a crop. We save more water with the use of drip irrigation. And unlike in conventional farming, the fields are not flooded, and many water containers are not needed too.

Better Nutrition: Fully ripe, just-picked vegetables and fruits contain more vitamins when eaten soon after harvesting, unlike store-bought produce usually picked unripe and have spent days or weeks before you bought it.

Five Practical Factors to Consider for an Edible Landscape Design

Asides the artistic aspect of the edibles landscape project, there is a practical aspect of it. Here are some vital factors you will need to put into consideration when preparing your edible landscape:

1. Microclimates

Know the parts of your yard or garden that receive the least and most sunlight. Most fruits and vegetables demand for at least six hours of sunlight daily during summer to produce more crops. Nevertheless, several edible plants thrive in the shade too. Some edible plants will flourish in any conditions imaginable. For example, in the spring, Ostrich ferns yield delicious fiddleheads while also grow well in full shade spots and in damp. Many edible greens thrive in part-shade to full-shade; examples of such greens are chervil, kale, vitamin greens, chicory, and lettuce.

2. Water Source or Sources

Where are the sources of water for your garden or yard? The water source can be rainwater catchment, an irrigation system, pond, hose, spigot, or other dry seasons' moisture supply. It is imperative to plan this and ensure a constant water source so that your edible landscape stays well-moisture all year-round.

3. Existing Soil Conditions

Which spots in your garden or yard have the most problematic soils? Sandy, dry, too wet, polluted, compacted, rocky, and so on. Each of the spots must be considered and make efforts to solve these problems or place the garden somewhere else.

4. Accessibility without Stepping

Do not step in a bed! Part of the conditions for having high-quality soil and perfect garden design is to in no way need to step on the dirt or bed to tend to plants (planting, watering, weeding, harvesting) or any other reason.

Every bed must be built as a single-reach bed (approximately two feet wide and used against fences, walls or other blockades) or double- reach beds (about four feet wide), or as long as your hand will reach the center of the bed from all sides.

Large planted beds that are wider than four feet must include stepping stones or hidden paths that make use of single or double-reach measurements for you to access every side of the landscape without having to step on the soil. You must also be able to identify and efficiently utilize your allotted stepping areas so that you are not just walking on the bed.

5. Type of Plant

What kinds of crops do you intend to grow? Nearly all edible plants love either meadow environments (for example, nearly all annual veggies grown from seeds) or a forest (for example, understory perennials and woody shrubs).

It is important to note that most forest plants will be in their best form well when a tree falls, and as a result of the canopy gap, they have access to full sun for a few years. Your beds can be designed to mimic these preferences for more substantial production and healthy plants. For example, you can place your meadow beds in the full sun using light mulches of leaves and straw and your forest beds in part to full sunlight with heavy wood chip mulches.

Once you have considered these five factors, every other step is hitch-free.

How to Get Started

You do not have to become an artist or expert at drafting a landscaping plan before designing your garden. Some people will draw out a comprehensive design plan while others only sketch out some points on a piece of paper and then gazed at it the moment they reach their garden. You can get a standard landscape design and swap the plant in it with edible plants. This is another excellent way to create an edible landscape design.

Analyzing Your Property, Gardening Goals, and Personal Tastes

To design a garden of your dream, you will want to inspect your current landscaping state. Remember to consider any setback elements added to your dream garden: this means you need to include things you do not want in your edible garden to the plan notes, probably, a runaway weeds frustration. Then, begin with surveying your land in its present condition (not what you intended).

You may also consider animals; they add a lot of different dynamics to edible landscapes but need further planning. Chickens and ducks can easily damage (for example, scratch, trample, or eat) most edible plants, so careful monitoring and fencing are crucial. Nevertheless, the pest insect control, improved soil fertility, and eggs they produce, qualify them as an addition to a garden environment.

After that, ponder things that matter to you (your defined goals). Your aims and objectives for your edible landscape will determine the changes you will make on the current state of your property. This is right as your edible landscape plan can include any of your needs and preferences.

After you have done surveying your existing property and your goals checklist, the next step is to start designing. The idea thing is, to begin with, the "problem" area.

One of the design principles in permaculture is that, "the problem is the solution". Check your list and think about those things you envisage as problems. When you keep those problems in mind dwell on what may be a permanent solution, and you will have a "Eureka" moment.

Possibly you will choose to plant espaliered apples alongside that chain-link fence to put your unattractive view out of sight. Or you will understand that shifting your vegetable garden from the far back of the yard to the narrow piece down your driveway's side (that you see every day as you wander the garden). This will allow you to notice weeds quickly while they are still small and before they take over all the places.

Suddenly, plucking the weeds becomes a way to unwind as you walk the garden after the daily stress or the blot on your landscape is covered practically by edible attractiveness. "Problems" make us think deeply and mostly bring out the most exceptional design elements in our gardens. So, the problems can turn out to be the solution!

Kudzu and bamboo can be serious problems, but they could as well be a great solution if you would like to make trellises for climbers like gourds, cucumbers, beans, and others.

Designing Your Edible Landscape

After analyzing your property, the next step is planning your style by asking yourself questions such as do I prefer an informal or formal garden? Do I want a theme- maybe Spanish or early Colonial? What about capricious areas with whirligigs or scarecrow?

Once you have determined your landscape arrangement, the next step is to choose the plants. This is where the true subtlety of the landscaper's lies. Begin by making a list of edible plants you prefer most and that thrive in your region, taking note of their cultural needs. Also, be conscious of their shape, size, flowers, and foliage color or fruit they produce (if any). Do you wish for tons of hot reds and oranges? Or maybe you would like a cooler scene with shades of blue, grays, and lavenders. Think about plum and apple blossoms, lavenders, and heady basils if the fragrance is essential.

Create areas of interest with your list of plants in hand. You can create a row of blubbery shrubs or a curved line of frilly-leafed chartreuse lettuce, which their glowing fall color could lead your eye down a brick lane and to your doorway. In place of the conventional row of lilacs along the driveway, envision a mixed hedge of blueberries, gooseberries, and currants. The possibilities are limited only to your imagination.

Here are Combinations of Plants That Would Inspire You:

Every plant in your landscape doesn't have to be edible. Think about the combination of the following colorful edible plants:

- A pathway surrounded by dwarf red runner beans against giant white-and-red-striped peppermint zinnias

- Orange or red cherry tomatoes growing over an arbor inter-planted with purple or blue morning glories

- A wooden planter brimming with burgundy-leaved cannas and strawberries

- A planting bed of fernlike carrots bordered with dwarf nasturtiums

- Yellow dahlias and gold zucchini surrounded by purple basil and zinnias

How to add a Unifying Theme to Your Edible Landscape

The next thing to take into consideration is a unifying theme for your edible landscape. This might seem quite non-natural if you are not naturally artistic, but trust me, putting up some kind of theme will surely please you beyond your imagination. Your unifying theme does not have to be deep or abstract, nor does it need to be anything obvious. The following are three simple suggestions for having a unifying visual element in your garden design

Consistent Hardscaping

Make use of a minimum one steady hardscaping object in every part of the entire landscape design. This is considered the most effective and efficient method of connecting your garden elements. You probably already needed plant trellises, edging, and paths, and using the same material for all or one of these is convenient. For instance, the existing rocks in your garden will unify the design while also possibly turn a problem of rocky soil into a solution.

What garden fences and trellises do naturally appeal to you? Bamboo, wrought iron, or painted lumber? Making use of your preferred material consistently in every part of your landscaping would give you your desired appearance.

Repeated, Continuing Plant Variety

Decide on a single variety of plant to repeat frequently all through your edible landscape. If possible, opt for a plant that flourishes all season long alongside a plant with a short season. For instance, you may decide to make use of disease-resistant roses for their edible rosehips, edible flowers, and beauty.

Another great, low-cost option is to stagger plantings of one variety or color of a long-thriving annual flower. Marigolds, cleome, cosmos, rudbeckia, or zinnias are some of the easiest in most climates. Any plant variety or species of your choice can be chosen for this purpose, whether perennial, annual, ornamental, or edible. Ensure to opt for a plant that will grow well in your region.

Color selection: Opt for a palette of colors or a single color to focus on in every part of your garden.

Bear in mind that no matter what theme you opt for, you will need to tweak it to be applicable to an edible landscape and to stand out in any condition. After you have done answering the above questions, coming up with needs, preferences, goals, and selecting a theme to unify your landscape design, you can now get started on your edible landscape. Cucumbers mountaineering a trellis to serve as a backdrop for a splash of coral gladiolus

As we all strive to contribute our quota in protecting our own health and the planet, looking for means of growing more of our own food is a laudable goal. The question is, how do you get started your edible landscape? You can replace a few shrubs with easy-to-grow salad greens and culinary herbs. Maybe the next step is to add a few rhubarb plants or strawberry to your flower border.

CHAPTER SEVEN: GARDEN DESIGN FOR CONTAINERS

he concepts of container gardening is simple, but there is more to growing plants in container than merely putting together a collection of plants. It takes a bit of creativity to have a garden that compels compliments from admirers. Your garden is not really a garden until it is well organized and well arranged, such that it gives an attractive look and a refreshing feel. Below are design tips you can consider and work with to create a beautiful container garden of your choice.

1. Your Choice of Container

The first thing to consider when designing your garden is your choice of container. The container you choose is one of the factors that determine how appealing your garden will be. These are the common types of containers and what you may need to know about them:

Terra Cotta: terra cotta containers are known to be non-resistant to frost, they are usually heavy, but a variety of them can make your garden visually appealing. They are not too expensive and keep in mind that unglazed terra cotta has good air circulation.

Wooden Containers: When you use wooden containers for your garden, their natural look gives your garden a refreshing holistic and earthy feeling. Proper maintenance is, however, needed to prevent the wooden containers from degrading. A recommended course of action is to line them with burlap or plastic and use low chemical sealers to avoid deterioration and damage to plants. After applying the sealer, ensure to wait for about a day before transferring your plants into the container.

Plastic Containers: These types of containers are lightweight, unlike terra cotta, and are sold in different varieties. Although they do not readily allow much air circulation, they can, however, be made to look like clay or other materials to give your garden a visual appeal.

Moss Containers: Containers like this enables you to grow plants through the sides and not only through the top. They are mostly used in hanging baskets.

Metallic Containers: These types of containers absorb heat readily and are recommended to be used only for heat-tolerant plants.

Other containers used by gardeners are milk jugs, bushel baskets, planter boxes, etc. It is important to use containers that can conveniently accommodate the root of the plant you want to grow and also give your garden the visual display you desire.

2. Choice of Color

The next thing to consider when designing your garden is the color scheme you choose. You could try out a monochromatic color scheme, analogous colors or complementary colors depending on the color of the container you chose.

Analogous Colors: Analogous colors are colors, usually a group of three colors that are close to one another on the color wheel. An example is a group of blue, blue-violet, and violet. Keep in mind that cool colors like blue are best fit for colored containers like terra cotta, and warm colors like yellow or red will go best with wood containers or, in some cases, terra cotta.

Complementary Colors: Complementary colors are simple colors that are contrary to each other on the color wheel. They are any two colors where one is the direct opposite of the other. Examples include a shade of blue and orange color scheme, red and green, yellow and purple, etc.

Monochromatic colors: Monochromatic color theme refers to different shades of a color. When you choose a monochromatic color, it gives an attractive look when a contrasting container is used to compliment it. An example of a monochromatic theme is a theme of purple shades – indigo, deep purple, lilac, and lavender.

75

Explore: You may as well creatively explore your choice of color for your garden. Go ahead and try out any combination of colors you want but ensure that it gives your garden an alluring effect.

3. Your Plants Arrangement

Plants arrangement is critical when you are designing your container garden. Usually, two ways of arranging plants within a container are according to their habit and according to their size.

According to habit: The terms used for plant habits are filler, thriller, and spiller. These three can be combined in a single container. While fillers refer to plants with mounding ability, thrillers refer to upright plants, and spillers refer to trailing plants.

According to size: Arrange your garden by grouping your plants according to their height. Arrange them in such a way that you have tall plants growing at the back and the small plants growing in front. Ensure that the groups of plant sizes you are putting together all complement one another.

Explore: You could as well explore and get creative with your plants. Try out plants with a variety of textures as spillers and fillers to make your garden design less stilted. You could also arrange your garden according to a similar pattern or function—for instance, herbs that grow well together, flowers with complementing petal colors, etc. Don't be afraid of exploring your creativity. You never can tell how beautiful the result of your ideas will be.

4. Location

The last thing to consider in ensuring a perfect design for your container garden is the location of your garden. As earlier said, your garden is not really a garden until it is well organized. You could turn anywhere and anyplace to your garden; the key is in the arrangement and organization.

Hanging Planters: If you are to use hanging planters, ensure that the background from where the baskets are hanging allows the plants' colors to radiate well. As a recommendation, using a white backdrop will help in achieving this alluring effect when the blooms from the several well-arranged hanging baskets start popping out.

Containers on the tabletop: You can utilize your outdoor furniture and place your containers on them. If they are well arranged and organized, they can give your backyard a brilliant attraction and a refreshing feel.

Depending on where you choose to create your garden, try to be creative with the arrangement. Utilize your doorsteps and stairs to create different levels of height and a general visual appeal for your garden.

CHAPTER EIGHT: COMPANION PLANTING

The idea of companion planting has been providing excellent results to the container farmers. It involves the planting combinations of specific plants for the mutual benefits of the plants involved. The concept here is that individual plants do help each other in taking up nutrients and helping with the management of pests, while also attracting pollinators. Nevertheless, researches are still on the way to find out more planting combination that works fine. There are a few that are listed here that have been scientifically proven and will also work fine in your container garden.

Melons or squash with Flowering Herbs

All the vegetables here are known to need pollinators for production. Therefore, you can plant flowering herbs such as fennel, parsley, and dill close to the squash or melon to invite insect visitors into your garden. The only way to get enough yields of these vegetables is through pollination.

Calendula with Broccoli

Calendula flowers are known to produce a sticky substance from their stems which in turn attracts aphids and gets them trapped there. Planting them next to brassica crops such as the broccoli will help to deter aphids from broccoli while also attracting beneficial ladybugs to dine on the aphids.

Radishes with Carrots

Both radishes and carrots take up nutrients from different locations in the soil, so they do not compete for nutrients or other resources. Their fast growth characterizes radishes, and they do not grow as deeply as carrots do. Carrots generally have long taproots, and it takes more time for them to mature when compared to Radishes.

Lettuce with Tomatoes or Eggplants

These plants are characterized by different growth habits which makes them beneficial to each other. Tomatoes and eggplants will generally grow taller; thereby, they are useful in shading cool-season crops like lettuce that doesn't like heat at all. Growing them with tomatoes or eggplants will also help in extending their harvest period.

Nasturtium with Cucumber

This combination involves introducing both pollinators and beneficial insects into your garden, which will, in turn, help in improving biodiversity. Nasturtiums are characterized by a unique scent that helps in repelling pests and also growing in a colorful tumble underneath.

Tomatoes with Basil or Cilantro

Apart from the belief that planting basil alongside tomatoes helps to improve the flavor of tomatoes, basil also has a strong scent that helps to prevent pests. As an added advantage, when basil or cilantro is allowed to spout flower, it will result in bringing in the pollinators.

Corn, Pole beans with Squash or Pumpkin

These combinations are popularly referred to as the three sisters. Corn gives pole beans a platform for climbing while beans will convert atmospheric oxygen into a form that can be used by both plants. Squash and pumpkin are leaves spreading plants, thereby creating living mulch that helps in reducing weeds as well as holding of moisture.

Lettuce with Chives or Garlic

Planting of chives or garlic, which is characterized by strong smell will help in repelling aphids, thus protecting your Lettuce. *You can* also add alyssum nearby to help invite beneficial insects.

Sweet Alyssum with Swiss chard

Alyssum is an annual crop that can be quickly grown from seed between the rows of vegetables, and it is known to attract hoverflies. The Hoverflies are beneficial insects that help in the control of aphids.

Chamomile with Cabbage

Chamomile helps in inviting beneficial insects for a variety of brassicas such as cabbage. You can cut off the Chamomile and leave to get decomposed on the bed while allowing the roots to remain intact to decay and help add nutrients to the soil.

Roses with Geraniums or Chives

Generally, plants that exhibit strong smell or taste will help in deterring aphids and beetle. Though it has not been entirely proven that this works, it worth trying to prevent roses from being eaten by beetle or aphids that multiplies rapidly.

CHAPTER NINE: TIPS FOR
GROWING VEGETABLES

Choose the Right Location

Choosing the right site for your garden is very important. A sub-par location may lead to sub-par vegetables. Below are a few tips for picking the right place:

Plant in a Sunny Location: Nearly all the vegetables need not less than six hours of direct sunlight per day. When vegetables receive enough sunlight, Farmers will enjoy a greater harvest, larger veggies, and better taste.

Plant in Good Soil: The roots of plants penetrate soft soil more easily, so try to get fine loamy soil. Then, enrich your soil with compost to provide the necessary nutrients. Appropriate drainage will make sure water won't collect on top and don't drain out too quickly.

Plant in a Stable Environment: Avoid planting in a site that tends to dry out a lot or location prone to flooding during heavy rains. Also, avoid planting in a place where strong wind can knock down your young plants or disturb pollinators from getting the job done. Plant your vegetables in a place where Goldilocks would be proud.

Choosing a Plot Size: Start Small!

Bear in mind that it is better to be proud of a small garden than to get frustrated by a large one.

Planting more than what you could ever want or eat is one of the most common mistakes that most newbie make. If you do not wish to have plants taking up residence in your tower, carefully plan your garden, begin small, and only grow what you will consume.

An ideal size vegetable garden for a beginner is around 16 x 10 feet (or less than) and features easy to grow crops. Based on the suggested vegetable in this guide, this plot size can feed a family of four for one summer, with some leftover for freezing and canning and giving to your neighbors.

Let your garden be 11 rows wide, and each row should be 10 feet long. To take full advantage of the sun, let the row run north and south. Cabbage, spinach, carrots, turnips, rutabagas, beets, beans, radishes, lettuce, and kohlrabi are some of the vegetables that can produce more than one crop per season.

After you must have chosen the proper location, the following tips will help you grow your preferred vegetables:

Space the Crops Properly: Corn, for instance, require ample space and can outshine shorter vegetables. Crops place too close together compete for nutrition, water, and sunlight are more vulnerable to pests and disease; and fail to grow well. Follow the spacing direction on plant tabs and seeds.

Make Use of Good Seeds: Individual plants are more expensive than seed packets, but if seeds do not sprout, your time and money are wasted. The money spent in spring for the year's seeds will be recovered in multiple with higher yields and greater harvest.

Water Properly: Watering your vegetable righty will provide them with the best possibility of producing well-formed, full-grown crops.

Plant and Harvest at the Appropriate Time: Do not plant too early or too late. All Plants have their respective planting date, so make sure you check the seed packet to know the planting date of the vegetable you intend to plant.

Here are Suggested Vegetables for Beginners:

The following suggested vegetables are common fruitful plants that are quite easy to cultivate. Consider it necessary to contact the Cooperative Extension Service in your state to discover what plants thrive best in your locality, and when best to plant them. Consider what you desire to eat and what is rarely available at the farmer's market or grocery store.

Top Ten Vegetables

- Tomatoes

- Zucchini squash

- Peppers

- Cabbage

- Bush beans

- Lettuce

- Beets

- Carrots

- Chard

- Radishes

Growing Tomatoes

Tomatoes are long growing, heat-seeking, and sun lovers. They don't tolerate frost as they are warm-season plants. The soil isn't warm enough until April or May in most regions, depending on where you live. The question most people ask is how long it does take to grow tomatoes. The days to harvest is depending on you, but the days to maturity range from 60days to over 80days.

Because of a long growing season, most gardeners prefer to transplant tomatoes than planting the seeds directly into the garden. You can purchase transplants in the garden centers. Choose short, stocky plants that have dark-green color and straight, sturdy stems. Do not use plants with stress damage spots, or yellowing leaves. Also, do not go with plants that have flowers or fruits already in progress.

Types of Tomatoes

There are a wide variety of tomato sizes, from small grape-sized to large beefsteaks. Your choice now depends on how you intend to use this versatile vegetable in your kitchen. For instance, Roma tomatoes are delicious in ketchup and sauce, but aren't very pleasant when consumed fresh. Tomatoes are classified based on their growth habit:

Determinate tomatoes are those that grow to a predetermined height. These types make a perfect choice for sauce making and canning.

Indeterminate tomatoes increase in height all through the growing season due to the fact that the stem's terminal keeps producing foliar growth instead of setting flowers. These plants continue producing fruits right through the season along with the plant's side shoots. So, if you would like to extend the harvest over a long period, the best choice for you is indeterminate tomatoes.

Tomatoes do need thorough care because the vegetable is vulnerable to diseases and pests. If possible, select disease-resistant cultivars to avoid troubles.

When Best to Plant Tomatoes

Most gardeners start tomatoes from transplants or small plants that they buy in the plant sales outlet because beginners don't find it easier starting by seed. Nevertheless, if you intend to grow tomatoes from seeds, start indoors six to eight weeks prior to the last spring frost date. Transplant seedlings when the soil is warmed that is, after the last spring frost date.

Before Transplanting

Two weeks prior to transplanting your vegetable plants outdoors, dig into the soil about one foot deep and mix in aged compost or manure. Learn more about preparing the soil for planting—the hardening off of transplants or seedling for one week prior to planting in the garden. Place young plants outside in the shade for a few hours the first day, steadily extending the amount of time the plants spend outdoors daily to allow direct sunlight.

To avoid damage of roots over time, set tomato cages or stakes in the soil during planting. Caging helps the plants to stand upright, while staking keeps tomato germinating fruits off the ground. To prepare stakes, make use of sturdy pole no less than 8 feet tall and an inch in diameter. Position the pole one to two feet deep and about four-inch away from the plant

Remember to choose a location with full sun. For Southern regions, light afternoon shade will protect the tomatoes from harsh noon sun and help then grow well. For Northern regions, make sure your chosen location receives no less than 6 hours of sunlight per day.

Tomatoes will thrive in different types of soil but must drain well and never pool water. To some extent, they love acid soil with a pH of 6.2 to 6.8

Planting the Transplants

Apply two to three pounds of a complete fertilizer, for example, 5 – 10 – 5, 10 – 10 – 10, or 6 - 10 – 4 per 100square feet of garden area. Avoid applying high nitrogen fertilizer like the types recommended for lawns. Too much nitrogen will encourage excessive foliage but will hold back flowering and fruiting.

For larger tomato plants that will be staked or small bush-type plants, space the transplants two feet apart. For larger tomato plants that will not be staked, space transplants three to four feet apart. Leave four feet between the rows. Remove some of the lower branches on transplants and place the plant's root ball in the ground deep enough so that residual lowest leaves will be just above the soil surface. If the transplants are long-limbed, bury up to 2/3 of the plant, together with the lower leaves. The stems of tomato can grow roots from the stems that are buried. Make sure you water the transplants well to create a perfect root and soil contact and avoid wilting. You may need to shade newly sowed transplants for about a week to avert undue drying of the leaves.

Tips for Growing Tomatoes in Containers

- Make use of a large container or pot that has a drainage hole in the base.

- Use loose, well-draining soil.

- A high-quality potting mix that has added organic matter will be just fine.

- Do not plant more than one tomato plant per container.

- Select from dwarf or bush varieties: most cherry tomatoes thrive in containers.

- You may need to stake the taller varieties.

- Put the container in a place that receives six to eight hours full sun daily.

- Maintain the soil moisture by checking daily and providing additional water during a heat-wave as pots tend to dry out quicker than the garden soil.